You Are No Longer in Trouble

You Are
No Longer
in Trouble

Nicole Stellon O'Donnell

White Pine Press / Buffalo, New York

White Pine Press
PO Box 236
Buffalo, NY 14201
www.whitepine.org

Publication of this book was made possible, in part, by public funds from the New York State Council on the Arts with the support of Governor Andrew M. Cuomo and the New York State Legislature, a State Agency, and with the support of Robert Alexander.

Cover by Jennika Smith.

Printed and bound in the United States of America.

ISBN 978-1-945680-24-3

Library of Congress number 2018947145

ACKNOWLEDGEMENTS

"Marriage" appeared in *Alaska Quarterly Review.*

"Staff Meeting Announcing Cuts" and "Afternoon" appeared in *English Journal.*

"The Bossy *e* Meets His Match" appeared in *Diode* in a different form.

"At Least Name It What It Is" appeared in *Tahoma Literary Review.*

"Broken Arm" appeared in *Watershed Review.*

"In Gratitude to the Dream Sequence," "The Principal Can Go Fuck Herself," "On Envy" (as "Class Discussion Three"), and "Second Grade Pain" appeared in *Passages North.*

"Landscape with Playground Equipment, Pigtails, and Hypodermic Syringes" and "Requiem for High Stakes Testing" appeared in *Crab Creek Review.*

"In Winter Even the Light Comes Late to Class," (as "One Classroom Window"), "What Everyone from This Place Already Knows" (as "Through a Different Window"), "What Not to Say to Your Students in the Juvenile Detention Center," and "You Are No Longer in Trouble" appeared in *Connotation Press: An Online Artifact.*

This manuscript would not have been possible without the generous support of an Artist Fellowship from the Rasmuson Foundation, a Boochever Fellowship for Emerging Artists, and an Alaska Literary Award from the Alaska Arts and Culture Foundation.

I am grateful to the U.S. State Department, The U.S. India Educational Foundation, and the Fulbright Foundation for the support of a Fulbright Distinguished Award in Teaching, which allowed me to travel in India and observe schools there. Although my time in India is not directly portrayed in these pieces, this manuscript was conceived during my time there. I have deep gratitude for the gift of that time away from my own classroom and for that travel, allowing me to view education globally, which transformed my perspective on teaching and learning in the United States.

—for my father & for my students

TABLE OF CONTENTS

I. Equal and Opposite

II. Each Time You Ask

III. Ignore All Alarms

I.

Equal and Opposite

Each One, Every One

For the walk into the ocean, legs heavy with muck. For the shotgun blast. For the rifle. For the Glade aerosol huffed behind the AC store. For the circle of boys who stood by watching. For the mystery of drowning. For the time it takes to find a body. For the bodies never found. For the ice, too thin this winter. For the dark. For numb hands, for blood tests. For the doctors who failed against the body. For neuropathy. For disease. For surgery. For accidents: the car accident on the way to school, the car accident on summer vacation. For the crosswalk and the crushed bike. For a friend's father's gun, loaded, unlocked. For watery cravings. For the soldier who made it only so far away. For the ones who never come back. For need. For the nod. For the cold of the stoop at forty-below, the five step climb too much. For hunger. For the dark hollows, the crooks of elbows and knees. For the name spray-painted in memory underneath the Cushman Street Bridge. For the water line above it. For the river's surface below it. For that river, so difficult to cross. For a name a mother chooses, syllables shaped on the tongue, still tart, startling. For that day in the classroom when you were still unlost. For the me who didn't yet know. For any teacher who ever said: *That one. Yeah, someday dead or in jail.* For *that* one, again and again. For each one, every one, now lost.

Afternoon

After gym. After library. After waiting and running and worksheets and waxy SRA reading questions. After the numbers squirm on the page. After the visit to the Enrichment Learning Center. After lunch, trays scraped into trash, the whole can full of brown paper bags. After Mrs. Barens tells you to stop chewing your hair, stop eating erasers. After she asks if she can give you a cracker from her desk instead because she doesn't understand the secret of eraser-grit on teeth. After tapping your pencil, tapping your fingernails, tapping your feet. After all that, she shuts off the lights. Opens the storybook. Sunlit dust motes float in front of the window. You put your head down on the cool of your fake wood desk, stretch your arms to the edge, then listen.

In the Winter in Fairbanks,
Even the Light Comes Late to Class

On Monday in December the sun rises at 10:40. Red sky. Black clouds. Among all the slouched backs, curved necks, and notebook-scrawling hands, only one student notices, a girl, the one writing about the room in which her mother died. She says, *I have never seen a sunrise like that*, and twenty-eight other heads look up from their pens and notebooks. I had never and will never again read a description of a hospital bed like the one she was writing at that moment. Years later, she will email to ask if I have *that piece* she wrote about her mother, and I will have to tell her I don't. But this morning, neither of us can foresee this future small grief. So I stop class while all twenty-nine line up at the windows to watch the light. Fifty-eight eyes open out onto snow, the parking lot, the shovel-scraped sidewalk, red brake lights, dull frosted stop signs. Red sky and burnt clouds. This morning, deep winter, sunrise comes, hours late, long after the tardy bell and without excuse.

Excuses for the Principal

— for my father

1.

I never told you about the candy. In your secretary's desk in your office where in the afternoons I waited, so small, too young for your school, pigtails pulled high, body constructed entirely of knees and squirm. To me you had real power, ties and suits in a musty-smelling closet so deep I could crawl to the back and hide. Power so strong grown women hid candy from you. Candy they'd sneak me while I perched on the vinyl green chair with metal arms, swinging my feet, savoring each sweet secret.

2.

You told me never to become a principal. Principals get only the worst parts of teaching. *Don't do it,* you said when I was student teaching. *It's not worth it.* And I remembered being small at the junior high school production of *Bye Bye Birdie* where I eavesdropped on two boys talking about you, about *Mr. Stellon,* a man I didn't know. They called you a name I don't remember. Something beyond second-grade cruelty, beyond my yet-to-be-developed vocabulary of opposition. The chorus—*What's the matter with kids today*—burned into my memory as I seethed, staring into the backs of those boys' heads. *How dare they say something so mean about my father?* Still only a teacher so many years later, I don't have to tell you I listened. Still a classroom teacher, I took you at your word.

False Lisp

Because the visiting speech therapist gave out stickers and your teacher never did, you pretended for two weeks to have a lisp. No one made fun of you because it was only third grade. Because you refused to stop pretending, one afternoon your teacher let you go to speech therapy, where the woman with bright make-up, the one who arrived each week in heels and a skirt, fancier than your plain teacher, gave you stickers. She leaned her elbows on the table, smiled right into your eyes and asked, *Are you pretending?* You whispered, *yes*, but she still let you take your stickers. You walked back to the classroom, brown shoes squeaking on the speckled checkered tiles the whole way.

The Fourth Person

— for K.C., a 10th grader who asked, I get first, second, and third person, but who's the fourth person?

I wish I had told him that the fourth person is always in line one person behind you, and they're obscured. Think movie extra, but pixelated. Everyone's impatient for the groceries to advance on the conveyor belt. The first person's cart is still in the way, and the second person is pulling vouchers out of her wallet, chatting, shifting, a squalling baby in her cart. It goes like this: One talks about herself, one thinks about himself, while you judge them both. None of you notice the fourth person, the only one watching the green-aproned cashier slide the groceries over the scanner. All that cashier wants: a break, a basket unpacked, just one customer who might look at her face instead of the flashing numbers on the screen. But even the cashier can't see past the third person. The fourth person, tired of waiting, leaves in search of a shorter line.

Marriage

The rash of weddings at recess continued until Mrs. Provencher had to give a talk. *You are third graders. You cannot be married.* Parents had called to express their concerns. The margarine tubs full of violets in your desk were bouquets and the flower girls had carried them, stems pressed into foil pilfered from the kitchen drawer. She can say what she wants, but you were married to Doug M. all those years ago, bound by asphalt promises over the screech of the swings' metal chains.

What Everyone from This Place Already Knows

—Togiak, Alaska

I should have known that the rotting walrus would be a problem, and I should have known not to take the dog to the beach again after he rolled in it the first time. I watched him: feet up, spine pressed to skin-rot and fat-rot, dog tongue joy-flapping out the side of his mouth. I didn't learn from watching that first time.

Everyone here knows only white, dog-walking teachers walk that stretch of beach, past the squat village houses against the gray sky, past the aging school with CRIPS painted on the side, past the round house where the herring fisherman come to stay in season when boats buzz the bay and helicopters pass over low. It's not herring season.

It's school season, and already two teachers and two counselors from the lower forty-eight have abandoned their contracts and flown home. Everyone here knows teachers come in the fall and leave in the spring. The opposite of tundra swans.

It's winter, and the swans are gone, so the teachers are here. That's normal, but the bay's not even frozen, so low tide returns the walrus to the beach no matter how many times high tide tries to carry it away. Stink stronger than low tide, stronger than the chemical smell in the once-on-fire ATCO trailer that serves as my classroom, the smell that lingers in my hair at the end of the day. Stronger, of course, than the grapefruit liquid soap I brought from Anchorage and the weak shower in teacher housing, stronger than the common sense once I swore I had.

Other Duties as Assigned:
Go Tell That Girl to Change Her Shirt

Somewhere in America there's a girl in a turtleneck weeping. But she's not the girl standing in front of the blue lockers in the hall outside the classroom where I've asked to have a private conversation with her.

Her spaghetti straps violate the dress code I've been reminded to enforce by a male colleague who's afraid if he tells her to cover up, he will call attention to his noticing her bra straps. Instead he calls my attention to my own bra straps, both tucked neatly under my own unflattering and professional blouse.

At the staff meeting, the principal asked women to be aware of their male colleagues' complicated feelings around this issue. *This is hard for men,* he said. *All the girls need to do is cover up. That's not difficult, is it?*

Coverage. Coverage of the halls, coverage of curriculum, coverage of her bra straps. And what's her crime, so young, so narrow, trying to learn her way into her body and algebra at the same time?

I look bad in a crew neck too. Boxy, middle-aged. That's expected, even encouraged. Otherwise the principal might say, *Cover up that cleavage. Aren't you too old for that shirt?*

Excuses for the Principal

3.

I never told you that I knew you thought I had killed myself that afternoon I fell asleep on the couch after school. The dead sleep of a teen up too early and to bed too late. Open mouthed, pale. You said my name in the language of your worst fear. I startled awake, sitting up on reflex before my dream even ended. *What?* I said, groggy. I could see it in your terror-drained face, but all you said was, *You scared me,* as you turned back through the door. I still see your shoulders in the doorframe, white dress shirt, the back of your head, your still mostly-black hair. I still feel my surprise—you had noticed my scarf-wrapped wrist, my self folding inward behind my closed door. I was afraid. You were afraid too.

4.

You told me when I was three I burned my left hand on a lamp in our living room. A light bulb round like the world. I sat for two days watching Sesame Street in front of the television, holding up my hand, and when it stopped hurting I forgot and held up my right hand instead. You watched me switch hands over and over. Again and again, this story. You told it to explain me to my self, too earnest and too dramatic at once, milking every hurt as long as I could.

In School, We Learn How Our Bodies Work

Miss Lashmet—pushing the whole of Hickory Creek Elementary toward the Presidential Award for Physical Fitness, pushing the girls toward our first tampons, first kisses, between braids caught in the scooter wheels and the Mexican hat dance competition—gets to present the film explaining how our concentrated girlbodies will someday work.

So much pink. So many flowers. The final image: red-haired girl, freckles and smile, insisting, *It's better than being a boy.*

Not really, says Miss Lashmet, rewinding the film before the credits even start. *Any questions?*

The buzz of fluorescent lights and the tick of film spinning backward answer, as the fan cools the bulb with a hush. No questions. Not even one.

The Bossy *e* Meets His Match

— for the reading teachers, with gratitude

e, nothing but a masked *c*, slack-jawed bandit, scrabbles on the roof of the train as the music swells. Below, through the dusty window, *o* and *a* cling to each other, skirts rumpled, mouths circled in a single terrified moan. At the back of the car, *e* kicks open the door, pistol poised, shouts, *Freeze! Empty your pockets.*

The train rattles on, a requisite close up: the bad guy's boot heel, each step, a thump doubling the dust. He was a playground bully, putting the *a* in shake. Now he has a shack, a hidden stash, a posse that has his back.

Vowels murmur, mutter, stutter, shuffle, drop their names into his sack while *x* unholsters, rises at the front of the car. Both feet planted, taking aim, *x* demands:

What sound does 'x' make?

e's forgotten, hisses, *Kiss?*—Question mark stuck just behind his teeth. Then he remembers the axe defiant, wedged in the block, hears the shot, lets the sack drop.

As if in a tunnel, the screen fades to black.

Staff Meeting Announcing Cuts

Immediately following the announcement that five teachers in the room will lose their jobs in May, the principal shows the suicide prevention video. Stammering assurances, he fiddles with his tie, presses play, steps away, and the woman in the video smiles, reminds us we can be prosecuted if we don't tell a parent their teen is suicidal. *Talk to the teen,* she says, *tell them there are other options.* In the reenactment, a boy gives away his driver's license as a gift, and I think about how, since high school, I have struggled to spell *license* correctly. For years, I looked it up in the dictionary. Now, I look for the red line under the word, whispering, *Error, check again.* Like the white line healed into the inside of my arm, whispering, *Look here, pay attention.* Once there was no word for cutter. Now, there's a video for that too. The woman says, smiling, *Tell them they could be a teacher someday,* and I want my bangs back, falling blackly into my eyes as I roll them. I want to pick my fingernails, pull the black scarf bandaging my wrist, look away and puff, *Teacher. There's no way I'm ever going to be that.*

Excuses for the Principal

5.

I never told you that day we went to the White Sox game together I soaked my face in Sally Hanson Creme Hair Bleach before you came to pick me up because I was afraid of what you might say. Longer than the eight minutes plus the additional five, so long my skin burned.

But before we turned the corner, you said, *You have a beard. Disgusting. How am I supposed to take you anywhere?*

Crying, I asked you to stop the car, told you I wanted to go back to my dorm. You pulled over, and we sat in silence as I wiped my tears with my palms and wiped my palms on my jeans. I felt your rage shaking the driver's seat. Baseball was our only safe subject. I couldn't imagine being a daughter to you without it. Would you go to the game alone? What would you tell my mother when you got home? I felt sorry for you. *How embarrassing,* I thought, *for your own daughter to turn down a ticket, a night game at Comiskey.* All I could say was, *Fine. Let's just go.*

Three days after you died, my mother, looking over the White Sox wall you made in the garage, asked, *Why don't you take that picture of you and dad with you?* The two of us framed in front of the scoreboard. Smiling, our matching brownblack eyes, my cheekbones a mold of yours. She meant to be kind, offering a memory you'd chosen to frame, one you'd nailed up among the jerseys and tickets. She meant to start passing on what you left behind. I felt sorry for her. What would she tell herself about that wall? About the blank spot that frame would leave? What would she tell herself if I refused? But all I could say was, *No, not that photo, yet. Not yet.*

6.

You never told me about your father. I found out one night when you were late at a school board meeting and our sibling-bickering pushed our mother to blurt, *Watch it or your father will end up in a mental hospital just like his father.*

We had a secret grandfather, alive, locked up? Unbelievable. She told me only these facts:

  1. He went crazy when you were two years old.
  2. His nickname was Fatty, but he wasn't fat.
  3. She thought your mother drove him crazy.

I used to imagine him in an old-fashioned straitjacket, a tiled room, sunlight streaming in. I used to practice in my head what I might say to him.

I used to wonder what Grandma Stellon thought. The Saturday nights we spent in her apartment on the Southside, I plotted how to ask her but never did. Her face the model of yours—which became the model of mine—frightened me, and the light of the black-and-white TV crowded my questions out of the room.

When he died, I was teaching in the village, where getting weathered-in or -out was a problem. Alaska was too far to come back for the funeral, and your mother was dying of cancer. I gambled to save my personal leave for her funeral instead.

On the phone, I asked the only question I'd ever ask you about him: *What was it like?*

You said, *A person I didn't know at all my whole life was my father. It was so strange to see him lying there.*

In Gratitude to the Dream Sequence

This will end when we wake, but at the moment we don't know the dragon isn't real and that the cliff is only three feet high. We're missing that the tiger behind the third door looks like our neighbor, but isn't quite our neighbor, and actually is our neighbor knocking on the door. It doesn't feel right, and it's not because the plane isn't crashing onto Mount Ararat where we'll find our accountant waiting with a bag of kittens and a yellow smock. We're not naked, and we really don't have a flamingo head for a penis. We're not flying and our hands aren't on fire. We have never won a fight with a robot. This time won't be any different. There's no reason for that coffee cup to have three handles. There isn't going to be a Mafia-style massacre in this restaurant in three minutes, so we don't have to run. And we're not having sex with her. No really, we will never have sex with her. And afterward, be glad. She won't turn into our principal and tell us we're fired.

Teaching Newton's Third Law in Juvenile Jail

— For every action, there is an equal and opposite reaction.

This morning the poet teaches science because the science teacher's kid has pink eye. But second period isn't biology, it's physical science. *Equal and opposite*, I think, noticing the brownness of my students in a town that's mostly white. *Equal and opposite*, I think, prepping a lab involving a medicine ball and a scooter.

In the textbook, dead Europeans with time on their hands drop things off towers. Some were jailed. Some not. All of them exist on the white page, unforgotten.

In the experiment, the students throw the 20-pound medicine ball to me and I throw it back to them. Then two students throw it to each other. Back and forth. When the weight hits them in the chest, they roll backward. When the same ball hits me in the chest, I roll backward too, but not as far because they know they have to throw more gently at me. Only because it is an experiment have they been allowed to be out of their chairs.

Equal and opposite, thinks the poet. *Each and every action.*

Lines Composed upon Finding a Note
Crumpled in the Corner at the End of the Day

Hey Marcella, so what's up? I want to tell you somethings so I am apologized about bad things. I want to be nice you so. also Jeff talked with you last night that is right? He just want to be solve with you so. Do you're glad that Jeff come over your house?

I do not know which of the 135 faces belongs to you. Too many swing in and out with the bells. Some offer hellos, some slump, some clutch books and smile, wide-eyed for attention, some only grunt. How can I know?

I do not know whose fingers gripped the Bic rollerball and pressed it into the page, who built the beautiful, sweat-rumpled, pocket-creased, blue-lined trash between my fingers, but I know whoever you are, student in fifth period, no matter your grade, your name, whether you were the one who called me *bitter old woman,* whether you told your reading group to fuck off, or you drew the picture of Gabe sucking a horse's dick, the one so high from huffing all you could do was stare at the pads of your fingers, or the one who puked in the garbage can in front of the whole class, whoever, I am solve with you because you, like me, are trying, for once really trying, to get just this one thing right.

Math Instruction in Late Seventies Suburban America

One morning in fourth grade, Bob S. called out answers aloud during the math quiz. He hunched in concentration, precise and correct, while on your page numbers jumped columns and quivered. His voice, a minor litany of perfect:

Forty-nine. Thirty-six. Twenty-four. Twenty-one. Seventy-two.

Forty-five and I still don't know what twelve times twelve is. Bob knows. I imagine him, fortyish, balding, as he recites numbers, tapping his fingers on the remote while I sit, still envious, graying, the too-fast numbers swimming the ocean of my keyboard.

Forty-five. Twelve. Ten.

Thirty-three years away from Mrs. Rebichini's classroom, from the hinged desks, from the thin girl I sat next to and resented for the way she could spell "melancholy." It's not that different. Admit it. Drills. Every day. The clock. The paperwork. Deadlines. Someone keeping time. Someone marking in red. But no one ever calls out the answers you're looking for.

Excuses for the Principal

7.

I never told you about the electrologist at the Gregory Hair Removal Clinic on Michigan Avenue, the one you made me go to after you said, *For Chrissakes, that beard is unsanitary and black.* The clinic I could walk to, near enough to the off-campus apartment where I once preheated the oven and a colony of cockroaches fled across the kitchen floor. You wouldn't have liked the aesthetician. She talked about the Nation of Islam as she buzzed and plucked my jaw. You had opinions about that. Only 18, I didn't understand your opinions, but I did know I deserved each bruise and scab. On the way back to my apartment from each prepaid appointment, I stopped to gorge at the greasy gyro place, then crouch and puke behind a pillar outside an upscale boutique. Had I told you I felt this way about my body, you would have told me, *Stop being goofy.* And then you would have walked away.

8.

You never told me about your childhood. My mother dropped hints in moments of frustration. As proof your mother was selfish, one afternoon my mother told me you never had new clothes as a child. *Just look at the picture in the hallway,* she said, dragging on her cigarette. *Even in black and white you can see the stains on his shirt.* I looked. You, the baby, third on the right, two steps down from your oldest brother's height, black hair dark as a matchstick strike. Proof: grease spots tracing their way down your plaid shirt. Evidence in black and white. She said your mother used all the welfare money to have electrolysis on the hair on her arms. The next time we visited, I gaped at my grandmother's smooth forearms in wonder. I wanted to ask what they once looked like, but I couldn't make the words.

On Being a Pregnant Faculty Advisor

I had much too much on my mind with my first pregnancy: miscarriage, maternal age, cytomegalovirus, nuchal folds, blood sugar tests. So at our after-school meeting, after the design and colors had been debated, once we were finally ready to place the t-shirt order for the Gay Straight Alliance's upcoming Day of Silence, considering the size my belly would be in April, I asked for an x-large without considering my students, and they all fell silent, until B., the freshman who played The Fairy Godfather in the skit they wrote together for the Diversity Assembly, the skit that led to day-long discussions over whether or not the Gay Straight Alliance should even be allowed to participate in the Diversity Assembly, said so gently, *Ms. O'Donnell, you really don't need an extra large,* with sincere concern over my self-image, and I knew it was time to tell them what was going on with me.

At Least Name It What It Is

Passengers in aisle seats lean toward the middle to watch the kneeling doctor's shoe bottoms facing us. It has been too long. His arms mark a rhythm we have seen on screen, felt in our chests, a rhythm that tracks the plane's arc into Juneau where we are not supposed to land.

Not-supposed-to began with the call: *Is there a doctor or an EMT on board? Please ring your call button.* Call buttons glowed, punctuated by chimes. Passengers strained to see, peered between seats, leaned into the aisle. Someone pulled a man from the window seat in row 11, dragged dead weight into first class. Metal hissed on curtain rod.

It has been too long. So long that screens flicker to life as some un-press pause. So long the flight attendant runs back twice for charged portable defibrillators. So long that we all know the answer without asking.

At touchdown, with phones back on, murmurs and beeps incoming, a woman three rows in front of me calls out: *Those who believe, pray for the one that is hurt.* The woman sitting next to me calls back: *I'm praying, sister,* and flips through a magazine full of recipes. Fingernails gleam over the glossy pages. Clatter of definitive pageturn. Amen.

My English-teacher self gets bothered by her word choice.

Hurt? Use *dead, suffering.* Hurt: an accident soothed by apology. Dead: definitive, done. If this is a prayer, it's going to go unanswered, so at least ask with precision. At least name it what it is:

Witness, not *bystander. Death,* not *medical emergency.*

In Juneau, one boy chirps and sings as his mother walks behind him, providing narration. *Now we will step forward to get back on the plane. Now you should look in front of you.* Her hands, a steady pressure on his shoulders. Her legs follow his lead in a stiff dance, holding him to this moment, down the jetway, down the aisle, back into his seat among his siblings, a few rows away from where the body once sat. She tells him everything is still real, how it is to go back.

In flight again, we become the dream-blurb of the body now stashed below. The doctor, arms tired from pumping, leans against the window. The man's wife takes her seat next to an empty seat and closes her eyes. The flight attendant dabs her eyes with tissue as she swings through the cabin, garbage bag sagging between her hands.

In Anchorage at two a.m., after we waited hours in Juneau, after we missed our connecting flight to Fairbanks, a chemo-ravaged woman stands quiet as her husband demands to talk to a person who can explain what we're going to get in return for our time. The customer service agent, exhausted, replies, *There is no person, sir. Only the website.*

I go to the customer service website. I write that I watched a man die on a floor with my headphones in and a comedy on pause. But I don't tell them the woman in the seat in front of me needed to get home that night because the dogsitter left that morning, and that she said, *I don't need to spend my one day of rest before going back to work cleaning up dog shit.* I don't tell them the Make-a-Wish Foundation girl with the prosthetic leg was on her way to see the aurora, or that I was flying back from trying to say goodbye to my father, who was dying himself.

Grading papers my first night home, I think of the flight attendant. How when she began the speech that batters itself daily against travel-dulled minds, her voice broke as she swallowed tears while her co-workers stood in the aisle buckling and unbuckling emptiness into circles of seatbelt. And how I listened to every word.

Excuses for the Principal

9.

I didn't tell you that the doctor said the baby might have Down Syndrome, that the nuchal fold was too big. You knew I was 22 weeks pregnant and that I had decided against an amniocentesis. You didn't know we were waiting until 32 weeks for a follow up ultrasound of her heart with the perinatal radiologist in Anchorage for another set of odds. For ten weeks you asked me, *How are you feeling?* For ten weeks I said, *Fine,* and cried, uncertain how I'd ever be able to tell you otherwise. Uncertain how you'd respond.

At the end of the waiting, the perinatal radiologist said her heart was fine. I didn't have to tell you. We chose her name on the six-hour drive back from Anchorage. I didn't mention it to you. When we decided she would be born at home, which was allowed because her heart was fine, I kept that a secret too. When you and my mother sent me a special robe you had chosen "for my time in the hospital," I said, *Thank you. It will do just fine.* I didn't tell you for what.

10.

You told me it would be so nice if we'd move to Chicago. *Just think of it,* you said, *you and your brother living streets apart, all the cousins playing.* My mother cried, *These granddaughters won't even know us.* I wanted to ask if you could tell I was happier, that I was doing better with my life here. But to ask I would have to admit I had been unhappy, which is not fine, so I said, *No, I don't think we could do that after so many years here.* That you could understand. *Yes, you're both vested in Alaska,* you said. "Vested" made sense to you.

Broken Arm

The teacher, all owly glasses and corduroy skirt, watches you stick a pencil in your cast, pull it out and smell it as you wonder at the minutes on the clock between now and when your mother will pick you up, cocoon you in the cigarette smoke of her Camaro. Your wrist doesn't feel like it's yours any more and you wonder if you'll recognize it. You wait for the moment in a doctor's office with a blade that can't cut skin but can cut plaster. How can it be sharp and not sharp? Cut but not cut? Once you cut your bare foot on glass on the front steps and you sat holding it, telling yourself the pain was only your nerves doing their job. That's what your teacher said about nerves. You thought once your brain knew you were cut, the pain would stop. After a whole summer's worth of swimming with your arm bundled in plastic bags and pinched by rubber bands, all you want to know is that knife.

II.

Each Time You Ask

Honestly

I didn't know you were a teacher. Oh, god, I'm sorry. High school? Not college? That explains a lot. I could so never do that. Thank god for you. You're a saint. What's it like to get paid for sitting around all summer? That must be nice. You get paid for summer, right? For glorified babysitting, imagine that. Did you do Teach for America? No. My cousin did. He's a financial analyst now. He says teaching was the hardest thing he ever did. He tells stories you wouldn't believe. Teachers don't get paid enough. You poor thing. It must be hard. Teenagers scare me. What do you think of vouchers? Aren't you afraid with all the shootings? With all the drugs? With legalized marijuana? With the texting? They can't even spell these days. How do you stand it? You should have a gun. When I was a kid it wasn't like this. My mother was a teacher. She used to pay us to correct papers on the weekend. What time do you have to get up? That's ridiculous. My kid hated high school, except for one class. I couldn't make her get up in the morning. I'm not even going to ask what you get paid. It's not enough. My son has the worst English teacher. Could you read his last essay and tell me what grade you would have given it? Just so I can compare before I talk to the principal. I promise I won't mention your name. Can't they just do school all online with games now? Kids today like that better anyway. Mine does at least. Someday we won't even need teachers at all. Teachers get paid too much anyway. What do you think of the school district here, honestly? No, honestly. Really? I couldn't ever send my kid to a public school. She would be bored. Nothing would challenge her there.

Excuses for the Principal

11.

I never told you the names we had chosen for our two daughters before they were born. It's not that I wanted to surprise you. I didn't want to hear your opinion. When we called to tell you we were getting married, mom said, *I'm not coming to some goddamn hippie wedding in Alaska. And your father will want to dance with his daughter. Don't disappoint him.* A compromise. A church wedding at the oldest church in Fairbanks. Years later, pregnant, I decided to make sure we wouldn't have to answer for anything else.

12.

You never told me that one day at the middle school where you worked, a girl left through the back door and was hit by a car. You had worried about kids running out that door, about the cars, the speed. You made announcements over the intercom at the end of the day. *This is Principal Stellon. Remember to look before you cross out back, students.* You rode in the ambulance and stayed with her body until her parents arrived. That night you must have come home from work late. Like every night, I was in my room pretending to be asleep or watching TV. Like every night, you never said a word. Your feet, a gathering of creaks on the staircase. Your hand running along the bannister past my bedroom's closed door.

In hospice, you were so grateful we were there—my mother, my brother, me. All three of us. As we tried to sleep on cots around your hospital bed, you kept raising you head counting. *One. Two. Three. You're all here. Even the other one is here.*

The other one? we asked each other.

After speech left you and you lay quiet, my mother told me she thought "the other one" was the girl who had died in your arms. A girl I had never heard of. A child you held and didn't hold as you held and didn't hold me. She said, *I think she's coming back to help him the way he helped her,* and then she went out to smoke. Unalone, I watched you lie on your side, and listened to the wordless quiet stirring around your bed, the pump's whisper, the stillness quivering deep in my own joints.

Proof

The father opens his parent-teacher conference by saying, *Now I know why animals eat their young.* He parks in one of the hard, plastic chairs his twin sons suffer every afternoon and fumbles with pages of grade reports and class schedules.

I don't know which twin he'd eat first. Twelve weeks pregnant, I spent the day teaching *Lord of the Flies*, thinking about boys and girls, awaiting results to tell me which I should think about more. I'm past the weeks of vomiting in the garbage can outside the classroom door without the class noticing, but I'm still terrified of every cough students bring through the door.

Do you have any kids? he asks. *No, but I'm pregnant,* I say. *Twelve weeks. My first.* He stops shuffling, looks me in the eye, says, *I'm sure yours will be nothing like mine.*

It's 7:30 p.m. I've been at work since 7:15 a.m. I'm tired. A book tells me that I won't feel the baby move for weeks, but my mother calls every day to ask, *Can you feel the baby yet?* She wants proof I can't give her.

But I can offer this tired father some proof of what his sons have been up to the past four weeks. So I open the file folder and begin to flip through the thick alphabet of last names.

Excerpt

—from a video shot to fulfill the requirements of the State of Alaska Department of Education's Teacher Evaluation and Recertification Program

Because teacher quality is the number one factor in student success, the state has decided I must film myself each year and submit a five-minute excerpt to someone in a basement office who will be trained to measure my effectiveness in the classroom.

Every student appearing on tape must have a permission slip signed by his or her family. Students whose parents refuse must remain quiet and out of the shot on days during which the class is being filmed.

My first video opens as the lesson begins, while students argue over whether pizza is a vegetable. It pans to the boy who had his extra pinky toe surgically removed last year because he wants to join the Army, where extra toes are not allowed. *It was really two toes, one budding off the other,* he says, untying laces as students lean in rapt. The girl with the note from her parents about having "sensitive eyes" wears clownish heart-shaped sunglasses, which she takes off to get a better view.

Thirty-four permission slips, I think. *I chose the wrong class.* But even I can't help but try to see for myself the scar where the toe once was.

Labyrinth

Because the Social Studies teacher notices you haven't been yourself, he writes a pass to counseling. Sophomore you: greasy hair, slept-in clothes you. The counselor's office, windowless, is lit with a table lamp, the fluorescent lights left off. Suburban Chicago institutional ambience.

She asks you things. Her head nods. Her David Bowie *Labyrinth* hair flops in perfect agreement. You answer a little, in that nail-picking-and-avoiding-eye-contact kind of way. In that teenage-caught-and-maybe-wanting-to-be-caught kind of way. So she asks again. You answer less or more, pulling at the black gauzy scarves you keep tied around your wrists to keep anyone from asking. When she suggests, *Maybe you should go to the mall and do a little shopping. That always makes me feel better,* and sends you back to class, she is just doing her job. Or whatever she thinks her job is. You can't blame her for not seeing what you work so hard to keep hidden.

Years later, watching a sophomore girl retreat into herself, noticing her sleeves pulled down over the heels of her hands, I choose not to write her a pass. I know her. I walk myself down to the counseling office, sit once again in the chair adjoining the desk. The same table lamp and the same box of tissues, the same institutional ambience shipped north to urban Alaska. I say, *Look, I'm worried. My student needs someone who's really going to listen.* I can tell she's between wanting and not wanting to be caught.

The counselor, with his close-cropped, George-Clooney, *Oh-Brother-Where-Art-Thou* hair, smiles. He has a suggestion. Without irony he says, *She should go to Young Life. The Christian group. They do wholesome things there—like milk-drinking contests.* He hands me a brochure for her. He is just doing his job. Or whatever he thinks his job is.

So I decide to talk to her myself.

Decisions Are Made

The parent didn't call me. Instead they called my Evaluating Administrator to say *Oedipus Rex* is a violation of their family values and that I said it would help prepare students for dealing with their parents. I don't remember suggesting that anyone model their family on the Theban family. It doesn't matter that what I said was it is a challenging text that will help prepare students for reading challenging texts in the future. I never get to say anything to the parent. They get to say that they looked online and the play has only an 8.5 lexile level of difficulty, so it's both too easy to read and has too much incest for a high school class. I never get to say it's in the curriculum. At parent-teacher conferences, the parent skips me and thanks a better teacher for being nothing like me, which the other teacher makes a point to tell me later.

With the support of my Evaluating Administrator, decisions are made. I will provide a different, less controversial book of equal literary merit, and I will no longer speak to the student directly. I am not to address the student in class, in the hall, or verbally in any way. Uncertain how I will choose said replacement text for the student without speaking to the student, I ask two questions. *No, they won't be switching out of your class,* and, *Yes, it is seven months until the end of the academic year.*

Nothing to Do but Listen

I practice paying attention to the student in front of my desk. The student whose parent made an appearance in the Public Safety Report this morning. The student who because they turned eighteen four days ago appeared on that list too. Named. Fleshed out as victim. Their voice floats over the empty desks, filling the space between newsprint names and the court-stamped papers to come. They tell me they plan to drop the assault charges against their parent. To stay safe, they will move in with a friend's family next week. There is nothing for me to do but be at my desk for them, to witness the moment they make words out of the words being made of the facts of their life.

Dear John Hughes:

You set high school in suburban Chicago, grid of white flight under the shade of trees lining tidy streets. Old trees, reaching across the street for one another but never touching. Cubs fans: shorthand for money and milksweet disappointment. Protagonist as smooth as the president's hair. An asshole, but an asshole with a good heart. Which meant everything else could be forgiven. You never forgave the principal, soggy-footed fool. You never forgave the droning teacher.

And you left things out. No racist playground chants. No rhymes. No comments at the family's all-white Thanksgiving dinner. You edited out the redlining, block-busting, contract buying, the history that built those suburbs.

You left out the pain. Where I grew up, no one mentioned that a boy and girl killed themselves on a farm road outside town on a Saturday night. A shotgun pact. His mother worked at a Hallmark shop that night. She restocked cards while he shot his girlfriend and then himself. She never came back to work.

No one filmed my first day of freshman year, when they assembled the entire class on the bleachers. If you were there, there would have been closeups: a nerd, a girl putting on lipstick, a jock. You weren't, so the principal simply said, *Look around. Four of you will be dead before you graduate. You don't want that to be you, do you?* And we looked side to side at each other, wondering who would be dumb enough to veer off the road, to embarrass our families like that.

Excuses for the Principal

13.

You never told me what it was like to stand in front of a class, that students notice everything. My first year teaching, in terror of the ninth graders noticing my beard, I went for electrolysis. I couldn't afford the thousand pinpricks of shame every Friday after school, but I paid for it myself. Scabby-chinned and swollen, I'd hide in the apartment all weekend before I had to teach again on Monday. You wouldn't have liked this electrologist either. She was a tall woman with a framed Mensa certificate, a deep voice, big hands, and a yappy terrier. I didn't think deeply about her, the only person to ever tell me to visit an endocrinologist, the only person to consider the role of hormones. I didn't think at all about her Adam's apple. Looking back, I realize you would have called her *goofy* too.

14.

I never told you I was angry you were unable to talk about your coming death. We had time, but no language. One night my mother called in a panic to put you on the phone. Hysterical after waking from a dream that something had happened to me, you wouldn't believe that I was okay until you heard my voice. I answered even though I was driving, stuck at a red light, with my sick daughter in the back seat on our way home from the doctor. I answered because by then any call from your number could be an emergency. I had a sick child, but I had to soothe you. *No, fine, everything's fine. We're fine.* Your terror, dulled by the miles of static between our phones, was the closest we would ever get to saying goodbye.

What Not to Say to Your Students
in the Juvenile Detention Center

Never say it. No matter how many times you've said it to other classes as thirty kids pack bags and check phones. Don't forget where you are now, post-job transfer and career change, post-background checks, post-confidentiality agreement, post-Prison Rape Elimination Act training. No one will *have a good weekend,* even if they earned all their points, even after Evangelical Christians, or therapy dogs, or the foster grandma who comes to play cards. The key lock box clicks and beeps approval as you leave on Friday afternoon. The swing shift is coming on. Not one of your students is going home. Never forget that.

Four Poems My Incarcerated Students Assigned Me

1. The Black Bear Speaks to Godzilla

— for T. K.

They built you of plastic and cloth in the studio, but I was here first. All you can do is lumber and screech, spit flames. They might fear you, but only in velvet seats, stuffing themselves with popcorn and forgetting who they are. But they know my paw skinned looks so much like their own hand: the hair on the back of their necks stands up. In the woods, one cracked branch implies a footstep. Just the thought of me makes them shiver.

2. The Devil Speaks

—for T. G.

I have more God tattooed on me than you. Believe it. More God in my Twitter. More preacher in my queue. More Bible in my belt. Let's prove this. They say I can quote scripture for my own purposes. I write scripture. You just don't believe me. Sometimes there's a voice, a burble behind the curtain of this moment. That's just Death and his brother, Sleep, bickering. Arguing over which one gets to visit you tonight.

3. Laughter is the Worst Medicine

— for J. I.

Go ahead, laugh at the video of another guy getting it in the nuts as his kid tries to break a piñata. You see it coming. He doesn't. That's it. Laugh. Falling down, falling off, falling over. It's all funny. Never not. Even without sound effects and the grating commentator. Look, the car is stuck. The car floats away. The car is on fire. The wall with men standing on top collapses. The tree falls on the house. On video it made a sound. He walked into a glass wall and it shattered. Or it didn't shatter. It doesn't matter. A man stumbles down the street. Look at him in cuffs. Look at him hit his head as the cop puts him in the car. You can't look away. Keep looking. Look again. Don't stop.

4. Abecedarian About Teaching
   in a Juvenile Detention Center

— for R. R., H. W., D. T., and R. G.

All my students come in sweatshirts as gray as morning.
Because no one has to wear orange, I know it was a calm weekend.
Color equals status, so I know everyone behaved or
Did what they were asked to do.
Every Monday, I'm refreshed.
Fridays I get to
Go home and forget the no
Home that's their home.
Inside, different air. Outside,
Just as I remember every day. Each one just a
Kid to me, since I don't know what
Landed them here. Full-spectrum lights,
Metal toilets upon which one student this morning
Not agreeing to come to class beats his shoe, an echo we can't not hear.
One shoe pounding out his discontent. Across the street at the adult
Prison, a former student, now 18, is being held. It was in the paper.
Quieted by new snow, the streets felt empty as I
Rolled into the parking lot thinking of him.
Seeing the door, entering the code
To retrieve my keys from the lockbox,
Underneath the buzzing lights, the buzzing doors, I want some
Value in redemption, but this morning
With the thrum of the
Xerox machine copying poems, clack of repeat and repeat, I think about
Young hands, crossed behind their backs
Zip-tied, mourning for losses to come.

Excuses for the Principal

15.

You told my daughters, *I bet you girls don't know how I got this scar on my middle finger,* as you began to tell them the only story from your childhood I ever heard you tell. A campfire, of course, the only one you and I ever stood around together, in my backyard with my daughters and a whole birthday party of nine-year-old girls roasting marshmallows. You said you used to hunt rats in the alley with your friend Charlie LaCocco and his dog Pal. Charlie stabbed you on accident while helping Pal kill a big rat. *He was a bad boy,* you said to my daughters. *Your parents would never let you run around with knives.* And my girls laughed and pulled out the pocketknives we had given them and they carried every day that summer. *We're from Alaska, not Chicago, Papa,* they said. This story is the only story I ever heard you tell about your childhood.

16.

You never told me what your mother did to you and your brothers. *It was bad growing up,* was all you could say. Once, I found a Dear Abby clipping in a drawer in Grandma's living room side table. Musty yellowed newsprint. A letter written by a wife whose husband had disappeared, asking Abby whether she should see other men or not. I can still see my small hands in the afternoon light of her apartment in Lituanica Street, the rough twill of the brown couch. *I have no grandfather,* I thought, *This must be about him.*

Punishment

Because Mrs. Deaney uses punishment as a way to teach cursive writing, you are not allowed on the playground this afternoon. *Open your mouth,* she said before she plucked the gum out with her manicured nails. So if you want any recess at all you must write *I will not chew gum in school* one hundred times as fast as you can. You try one word at a time. Vertical

I will not ...
I will not ...
I will not ...
I will not ...
I will not ...
I will not ...

Letters fall down the page like rain rolling down a window. Not fast enough. You are in love with a blonde boy, and you have to get to the playground to see him, chase him until he turns on his heel to chase you. Run fast, but not as fast as you can, knowing that he will grab you, drag you back to the boys' base where you hope that no girl will come to your rescue. Take three pens. Use four fingers. Make a claw of your hand, and you'll get three lines at once. Until your hand cramps, make cursive curl across the paper:

I will not chew gum in school.
I will not chew gum in school.
I will not chew gum in school.

Three lines at a time until the entire page is full.

An Incident at a Staff Meeting at Togiak School

— Togiak, Alaska

I shift in the small hard plastic chair in the seventh and eighth grade room. If it wasn't for the broken windows, there would be a view of the Bering Sea. The former principal mentioned the view in the interview. The one window that isn't boarded up lets in light polished smooth as beach rock. Dreaming of being on the beach throwing rocks into the sea, I don't pay attention to the meeting until the teacher-of-the-year science teacher stands, waves a baseball bat, and shouts, *We know who it is. Can't we all get baseball bats and just walk him into the sea?*

Like him, most of the teachers have been flown in from Outside. As an itinerant science teacher, he appears seasonally, visiting each village for twelve weeks at a time.

He swings the bat in front of the chipped green board. As if beating a drug dealer into the bay would be a sacrifice bunt. As if the drug dealer wasn't everyone's cousin. And I, the Imported White English Teacher, make significant eye contact with the Imported White Middle School Teacher and the Imported White Math Teacher before we all look down at our feet.

No one stands and scrambles for bats. No one moves. The first-grade teacher born in the village sits quietly and looks down in the same way she does when the principal talks. We follow her lead. When he storms out shouting, no one follows.

When it's all over, I wonder about so much, but mostly, where he got that bat. Did he bring it to every village he visited?

Landscape with Playground Equipment, Pigtails, and Hypodermic Syringes

— for T. J.

Yesterday afternoon under the slide, a stash of used needles, a dented coffee can. At least that's what the pig-tailed girl tells me. Imagine a squirt gun, hot afternoon sun. No water. No memory. No science class.

Some boys pissed in the can, filled syringes, gave chase.

The next morning, after the phone calls, after the meeting, after the email composed with care, at circle time I find myself asking them, *Why?* They are only fifth graders, I am only a teacher standing before them with the school nurse and her folded arms. They have no answer. No sense to be made. Not the playground. Not the nurse. Not the cross-legged boy crying on the bright colored carpet. Only the syringes, fallen in rune-like patterns in the gravel, a script none of them could read.

Writing a Clear Rubric for Class Discussion

She means what she meant to say, which is the problem. Which is to say that she's meaning not to be mean, but being mean is the problem. Which is to say if this poem is understood correctly by the reader, left standing out in the storm of the words that make no sense, and more words, just rain pouring down and no umbrella, no slicker, no cap, then it must mean something. She's afraid she's mistaken again, cloudy with water in the ear that causes her to tip her head to the side. In inverse proportion to her confidence in what she's meaning to say, her sentences lilt upward. *If the poet's words are water, which they aren't, is something meant by the puddle at the end of the poem?* No, that's not what she meant at all. Not at all.

Parent-Teacher Conference

The mother and father seem concerned, but they shouldn't be. The parents who should be concerned never show up to conferences.

I am not worried. I am the teacher. Look at the test scores. Look at his writing sample. He works well in groups. *Do you have any questions?* I ask.

The sad-eyed mother says, *Can you tell me what my son is like? He doesn't talk to us.*

Excuses for the Principal

17.

You never told us you were dying. *Fine, fine,* you were fine. You were always going to be fine. The surgeon barely told us. He said only, *Everything we do will be palliative,* hoping a poor vocabulary on our part would save him having to give bad news. When I asked, *So are you saying that you can't do anything curative?* he met my eyes for a second.

After the third surgery, after I listened to you screaming as he pulled out the staples, after you had settled into the ICU and met the night nurse, you told me that behind the bathroom door it was India, a market, just like the pictures I sent you. *Look at the colors,* you said. *Just open the door.* Before he left, the surgeon told us without looking into our eyes, *Delirium is not uncommon.*

So each time you asked, I re-opened the door.

18.

I never told you my first year teaching I'd cry on the edge of the bathtub mornings before work. You would ask, *How's work going?* and before I could answer, you'd interrupt with, *You're the kind of teacher I'd hire. You're a natural in the classroom. I can tell.* I learned it was easier to say, *fine,* so you wouldn't worry. *Fine,* I said. *Fine,* practiced and almost natural, like every shaky truth.

Projector

Years ago, there was a beep and a knob. Once a click, a strip, a whirr. The definitive pop of the filmstrip canister. A whizz, a hair across the screen wiggling. Black and white, then color. Then melting in the glow of a too-hot bulb. A burning smell. Giggles. A frustrated sigh.

Once I was the chosen one, fingers satisfied to turn the dial at each beep, to feel the fan's hushed buzz spreading the bulb's warmth across the desk.

This afternoon in my daughter's class, it's quiet. Headphone quiet. 32 kids, 32 screens, the rumble of video narration. Every ear plugged. Each press of pause and play re-syncopating the hissing buzz. They choose what to click. Every button catered to their budding desire.

III.

Ignore All Alarms

Drills

1.

In the days after *The Day After*, over the pile of paper bags covering the folding cafeteria table, we ask each other questions about the coming nuclear war. Someone shares facts she says her mother told her: A woman wearing a polka-dotted dress when the bomb dropped had polka-dots burned onto her body; people can vaporize; fallout looks like snow. We wonder: will our skin melt? Would it be safer to be curled under the coat rack benches in the hallway or upstairs on the second floor of the school? Won't the school fall on us? On the TV, people covered their windows with paper. I didn't understand: Could paper stop bombs from melting people? How? In a magazine article someone learned that the president with the shiny LEGO-man hair wants giant lightsabers in the sky to shoot the bombs down. I heard he keeps a jar of jellybeans on his desk at all times. I know how to curl myself into a bean shape under the bench. Because that is the shape we practice in the duck-for-cover drills.

2.

When the alarm goes off, none of us is surprised, because it's -30 and the principal sent an email mentioning the fire drill, so we all casually dropped to our students that they might want to bring their coats during 5th period. I say, *Oh my, students, hurry, a fire,* in a Willy-Wonka voice as I grab my clipboard to take attendance outside. We will not be allowed to go back inside until every teacher has turned in a correct attendance sheet. We must note who was absent, who was in the bathroom, who was out on a pass to the counselors. It's been drilled into us that the principal will be timing us. When a student asks, *Why do you have to take attendance?* I lie, say, *Because the Fire Marshal could fine me if my attendance is wrong.*

3.

Before I had children, I left my coat in the classroom, thinking it was better to be in the same boat as my students, bare-armed and freezing during a winter fire drill. How is it fair that all the teachers stand outside in their coats while students shiver? After I had children, I brought my coat, hat, and mittens, and handed them out to underdressed girls.

4.

A robocall, the principal's voice on the cell phone. *Yesterday the district received a credible threat on social media. Tomorrow we'll have a police presence in the building. We are investigating.* In the morning there will be an all-staff email. I've memorized the email after so many years. I know the drill. *Remain calm. Teachers set the tone. Share these talking points. Dispel rumors. Report anything suspicious.* Brushing my teeth, I ask myself the question I ask myself each time: *Would I throw my body in front of another mother's child?* I convince myself the answer must be yes.

5.

During the passing period, the teacher next door tells me to check CNN, that there's been a shooting in a first grade. I skip the bathroom and rush back to my room. As my students file in, I stand at the podium staring at my laptop. My daughter is in elementary school. Her father is her first-grade teacher, and I think, *If that was their school, his classroom is the second from the front door.* When the bell rings, my class stares at me. I manage to say, *Let's get out our notebooks,* and from there the muscle memory of classroom management carries me through second period. I think I did well, but on his way out a boy stops, touches my arm, asks, *Are you OK?*

6.

Another drill. More practice. When *Lockdown* comes over the intercom, I follow the steps. First, I look out into the hall for students without a hiding place. This morning, there are none to invite in. Because classroom doors lock only with a key on the outside, I smile and shrug at the teacher next door as our keys strike synchronized notes. After I'm back inside, I roll the curtain down over the window in my classroom door. Every door was built with a window because no teacher is allowed to be in a closed room with a student. Windows keep students safe from predatory teachers. Two years ago, in an all-staff email, the principal told us to uncover all doorwindows to protect ourselves from accusations. In lockdowns this year, we have been told to cover the windows. Doors with covered windows keep students safe from shooters with semiautomatic weapons. In the staff meeting, a teacher who is nearing retirement asks, *How do you want us to cover the windows that you so recently told us to uncover?* The district will not be providing materials. The principal suggests we use butcher paper from the art cart to make ourselves roll-up curtains. But we should be careful with the paper because the school won't be able to buy more when we run out. I use my prep time to make the curtain. When I'm finished, my roll-up curtain is black, and written in white it says: *When you stare into the abyss, the abyss also stares into you.*

7.

A teacher I've known for years confesses that in 1986, when she was in high school, a boy shot the substitute for her French teacher. Lunch discussion, classroom door propped open, students milling the hall. Because it's spring, we have the light turned off and the windows wide for air. *He was angry that he was failing, so he shot her in the head, but he didn't realize there was a sub that day,* she says. He went on to shoot the vice principal. She remembers stepping over the sub's body as she left the classroom. A student comes in to make up a

71

quiz and we change the subject. When she goes back to grading papers, I stare at the door's rectangle of light and imagine her silhouette taking careful steps over the substitute teacher's body as she tries not to get blood on her shoes.

8.

I'm having contractions, or what I think are contractions, as I stand in front of my third period class. I call the office, where the secretary, who has five children and seven grandchildren, can tell me what to do. She sounds panicked before I even tell her I'm having contractions, and when I do, she sounds relieved. Her relief leaves me relieved. She has had babies before. I have not. She tells me to leave and call my midwife. When I sign out at the office, she appears distracted, almost disinterested, as if I were leaving for a dentist appointment. As if I'll be back in an hour. This is my first baby, so I feel neglected. Even though the contractions turn out to be only Braxton-Hicks, my body's own drill for labor, I don't come back. I stay home to wait for the real thing.

Two weeks later, while I nurse my new baby, a co-worker calls. She tells me that while I was leaving the building that day, the hall monitors and principals were standing outside a classroom where a boy had a gun in his backpack. At the moment I signed out, they were deciding what they should do.

9.

I get one text when my daughter's school goes into lockdown. There is an incident. An incident is not a drill. I teach in the jail where no one has a gun, or a cellphone, or even a paperclip, but a man with a gun lurks in the vicinity of my daughter's school. I get another text when the incident ends. Schools call this "communicating with parents and guardians."

Later my daughter tells me about her day at school. They hid in the orchestra instrument room for hours. The teacher had a bucket and a blanket in case they needed to use the bathroom. When I express surprise, she tells me, *The principal made all the teachers get blankets and buckets for lockdowns in the fall. It was the plan.* The boys took turns seeing who could pee longest. *Only one of the girls peed,* my daughter said. *She really had to go.*

My daughter kept a log:

> *First half hour we thought it was a typical lockdown, laughing and talking. Now people are speculating, nervous crying, our death. Second half hour: people are freaking out and crying. We have been almost silent for nearly an hour. Bubblegum. Chopsticks. Ninja phones checked. Rock, paper, scissors. Half hour three: we have been reduced to peeing in a bucket. 20 minutes ago I acquired this pen and paper. Current time 12:52. H. wants her family to know she loves them very much. S. wonders what happens if you need to go #2. Mr. Lockwood is keeping us calm.*

While she does her homework, I read the news online. I learn the man had killed his sister, that he came to the front door of the school, that the staff turned him away. In an email later that night, the principal commends the teachers for their excellent work.

10.

Tomorrow the shooter could charge the lunchroom or pull a fire alarm. Next Wednesday the shooter could be angry about his grade, and next month obsessed with his girlfriend. One Friday the shooter could be lonely or sad. He might post online or call in a threat. By the end of the year we'll all have the chance to eulogize a brave, wise, anonymous friend. Or heroic teacher. And then a week later indict a fool counselor, a writing teacher who didn't read a journal in time, an art teacher who thought it was just a picture. Next year the shooter might be someone you know. No, the shooter will be someone you know.

11.

Educational consulting firms have begun selling school districts training modules for active shooters. Selling us exactly the same as the drills we've been doing since 1998, my first year teaching: secure the building, clear the halls, sit tight, lockdown, cover the doorwindow, lower the shades, call roll and note absences, stay on the floor, remain quiet, stay off the phones, ignore all bells and alarms. But now they also want teachers and students to practice throwing things at the shooter. For some thousands of dollars, their trainers will come in their company-logo polos and shoot blanks in your school hallways to acclimate students to gunshots. They will break into classrooms and have students whip company-logo stressballs at them, so students can learn to pummel active shooters with classroom detritus: staplers, tape dispensers, books, pens. They suggest you do a classroom canned food drive and leave the box in the room, so students will have cans to throw at the shooter.

12.

At fourteen I was terrified of red phones, pressed buttons, men in suits. Distant threats, bombs like thunder rumbling at the edge of the far cornfield. I crushed on Matthew Broderick playing a boy far too old for me in *War Games*. Such a beautiful boy, screen light reflecting off his soft brown eyes. One high school boy, alone in a dark room with his computer. Playing a game, he almost destroyed the world. But he saved it after all.

Thirty years have passed. The bombs rot in their silos, but threats aren't so distant. So many boys illuminated in screen light. It turns out no one needs a button or a red phone. I don't need a movie to imagine it. I have practiced. I have helped children practice. The boy stops right outside the door. A footstep, a shadow on the paper covered window. I don't understand: Can paper stop boys from killing people? Just hush. Don't ask. Follow directions. Stay off the phones. Ignore all alarms. If we all listen, close up, we'll be able to hear his finger ready on the trigger before he even touches the door. The drills have made us ready.

Morning Announcements

This morning the speaker crackles next to the wall clock, *There will be no more warnings about sagging pants, seriously! Zip ties will be used to tailor your waistline appropriately.* This is followed by the mispronunciation of names with flat congratulations, stiff reminders about deadlines, and unwelcoming invitations to the school book group: *This month we are reading* [insert another edgy, but not too-edgy young adult novel]. *There will be snacks!* In a few seconds, the students will be asked to stand and face the flag. I have thirty seconds to click attendance bubbles on the screen of my district-issued laptop. Present. Absent Excused. Absent Unexcused. I will not have another minute all day.

I Remember That Girl, in Third Grade, with the Perfect Blonde Hair

When I asked why you kept a black rosary in your desk, you described your mother's hands in her coffin, beads threading them together in permanent prayer. At eight, I had never seen a dead person.

Thin gold belts topped our tiny Oh-La-La Sassoons. You said, *If you wear a belt tight, it pushes the fat down and no one can see it.* I tightened my belt, sucked in my belly and believed. Your mother was dead. You knew grown-up truths.

In high school, at night I folded my hands together, shame burning my pressed palms. I believed death was a pose, and imagined the black rosary my mother would knit through my fingers. As I planned how I'd kill myself, my hands brought back your mother's hands, brought back your whisper between our desks as you leaned, hair brushing my arm, green plastic chair creaking under you. By then I didn't know you anymore, but I imagined your rosary as my mind imagined unhusking itself from my body.

Tonight, lying on my back, fingers twined across my belly, the shape of my body brought back the bruised me who wanted to die, then your mother, then you. I did what every forty-year-old does when a memory floats up, I googled. Your birthdate same year as mine, I found you living only one state away from our old school. In my head, I began writing the message I would send. Then I found your obituary.

Suicide. Three weeks ago.

I never asked you how your mother died. Half-formed and fuzzy, back then I didn't know that anyone, not a mother, not a friend, not myself, might want to leave her body behind.

Now I know. And I know you knew too.

Contract Language

Teachers will accrue six days of personal leave a year, but they may not take personal leave on the first and last day of the semester, the day before or after spring break or Thanksgiving, or on the day when there's a staff meeting, professional development, a presentation by a consultant, parent-teacher conferences, federal or state mandated testing, or a final exam.

Teachers may not take personal leave the day after they cried in the bathroom after work, after they taught sixth period despite the panic attack they had during fifth period prep when the Discipline Secretary told them they couldn't leave the building because there were no subs available. Teachers may not take leave when their fathers are dying, when their children have a performance at their school, or if they need to attend their own child's parent-teacher conference.

Teachers should save their personal leave for the Wednesday before quarter grades are due, but only if they were up until 2 a.m. grading essays and they've taken hours to write sub plans that no one will follow, so they can stay home and grade the essays they couldn't finish grading the night before. There will never be time during the workday to grade the essays needed to provide the detailed formative and summative feedback to students that is required on the teacher evaluation instrument, so teachers should be careful to use leave wisely.

There will be no sabbatical, administrative leave, or professional leave in the upcoming contract year. Teachers should contact their building's administrative assistant if they have questions.

The Principal Can Go Fuck Herself

Can't she. Isn't that what everyone has wanted to say. The principal, in her pantsuit and big necklace. The one who would become every boss you ever had. The one who doled out doling out detentions to the underprincipals, who were smaller, diminished. Like principals that had been erased and rewritten a little more crooked. Like principals that had been run through the wash. The Man with a lowercase *m*. Men. Or Women. Which is just an upside-down *M*. The woman principal was The Man. We should have called her The Headmistress. No one would talk to a headmistress that way.

Excuses for the Principal

19.

You told me the only hire you regretted in your career was Mr. Buff, who eventually became my seventh grade English teacher. The one who took us all on a bus to the state speech contest where I recited *The Yellow Wallpaper* and in the high point of my junior high career earned a first-level score. He was from downstate Illinois where people pronounced Cairo, Illinois, *Kay-Ro*, and Bourbonnais *Bur-Bonus*. You never told me what you regretted. Only that you regretted.

Mr. Buff hung out at Gracie's, the biker bar on Main Street. Once every few months, twenty Harleys would rumble down our street toward the bar. *It's on the biker circuit*, you'd tell me. Sometimes, on summer afternoons, I'd walk past the open bar door slowly, and side-eyed look inside. Gracie, an old woman, a gray poof at the bar and Mr. Buff's black biker boot, heel on the crossbar of the stool. The beer in his glass as blonde as his shaggy hair.

20.

I never told you that we didn't have ants in the kitchen. It was me eating everything while I was in middle school. After the bus ride, home alone, I'd eat the whole box of cereal, and tell you, *I had to throw it out because there were ants in it.* The Sara Lee poundcake. The whole loaf of bread. The chips. The bag of your favorite cookies. You'd watch me eat dinner, lips tightening as I reached for a slice of pizza out of the box. You never said anything. I imagine you knew. Or at least suspected, so once I could drive and had a job, I'd drive through and buy my own food after school. No one was home, so the purging was easy to hide.

On a Field Trip to View the Tourists at the Museum

—University of Alaska Museum of the North, Fairbanks

We came between bus-bursts, so at first the museum was ours. The museum, packed with taxidermied birds, prehistoric wood bison horns, and mammoth teeth, where each year the Upward Bound students went on a class field trip, where this year I had created writing exercises about the things they would see labeled and displayed, which means things that they had already seen in their home villages many times. Like the kayak stretching along a whole wall, or a video of whale hunters, or a video of Yup'ik dancing that featured a few relatives, now gone. And an arctic fox standing on a plastic snow bank that inspired one student to tell me about a rabid fox that was a danger as she walked to school one morning. Her auntie called on the VHF radio to warn everyone.

The museum where busload after busload of daily Princess Cruise Line charter coaches rolled in at scheduled intervals and unloaded camera-toting, gray-haired visitors for their allotted minutes in front of the displays and then in the gift shop.

The museum where we were alone, our small class surrounding a table of pelts—wolf, wolverine, ermine, beaver—and we were talking about hunting and uncles and parka ruffs, until a circle of tourists surrounded us. Tourists who hadn't yet learned the words *Yup'ik, Inupiaq, Athabascan, Aleut*, who buy round-faced, smiling, made-in-China plastic dolls in fur-ruffed parkas for their grandchildren, who had cameras and questions, who wanted pictures of my students holding the furs because my students didn't have plastic faces.

The museum where I, not yet a licensed teacher, not yet a mother, not even yet an auntie, bristled as a man asked one boy to hold up the wolverine pelt and smile. I don't remember exactly what I did, but think I said, *No pictures.*

I hope I said, *No pictures.*

I need to believe I said, *No pictures.*

I do know some of my students talked to some of the tourists for a while, while others left for a side gallery where the tourists didn't go. I do know I made a rule that for every question any tourist asked, they had to answer a question about their own personal lives from my students. I do know that we stayed for a while. Until the tour guide called them back to their bus. Until some of them realized they had missed the gift shop.

Walking back to the dorms, C. whispered to me, *Nicole, I met a Black man from Georgia. He didn't want to be in Atlanta for the Olympics. Why would anyone leave during the Olympics?*

I don't remember my answer.

I do remember the perfect pelts, the wolverine's black-white *V*, the afternoon sun, and our shadows dragging along the sidewalk between the museum and the dorm. And myself, so young, watching how history tangles itself around children's ankles and pulls them under.

Myself, the teacher, another tangle. Another tourist, deciding what to take back and what to leave behind. Still writing about kids that aren't mine and never were in a land that isn't mine and never was.

Requiem for High Stakes Testing

The teachers nod every time the consultant says "data." Their nodding is synchronized, practiced. Data means "nod now." I know what he means. He knows what he means. He means the means by which we will be measured have been changed. He's saying (without saying) that someone keeps moving the line, not him, not us. He's just here to draw the line. Something about not killing (or killing) the messenger. Someone behind me is kicking the hard plastic chair that's making my ass sweat this August afternoon.

Someone's in charge. Someone got paid. The consultant clicks a remote and the noiseless slide that isn't a slide disappears. A new slide, a comic. Something funny as a background for this announcement every teacher has heard: *Yes, that last test, the one you worked with and around for ten years, is not valid.* It never was. The one whose results were lauded or bemoaned every August. Remember that test, the acronym a choke-hold on the vocal cords, that denied diplomas to some unfortunate students every year for the past ten years? Remember when the legislature passed the law that required it? Remember when we revised the whole curriculum around that test? It's canceled, and beginning today the district will provide diplomas to all those students, whether they missed the cut-off scores by one point or thirty, but only if they write in and request them. Students with names and faces I remember. The consultant half-grins and mentions legislators, shaking his head.

But the new test, he says, *this one, the one featured on these slides, is valid.* Completely valid. Researched, bonded, sealed, legislated, approved. Someone new is in change. Someone new got paid. Isn't it great? Here's the data to prove it: the progress of students in another state, 2600 miles away. He clicks and another slide appears. Look: three year's growth in one school year. Look: eighteen month's growth in one school year. *If you could only see it for yourself, you would believe,* he says. Believe him. He smiles. He understands your frustration. He understands. Really, he does.

I understand, really, I do. I can see for myself, and all I can do is nod.

First Day of School at the Juvenile Detention Center

No one's mother took a first-day-of-school picture because mothers aren't allowed and every student wears the same Bob Barker clothes: Velcro sneakers and plain navy blue pants with elastic waists. All summer no one went home. Which means there was no summer. For them. Me, I had summer. I went home and slept in and traveled to places that required a passport. I planted a garden. It grew and became some of the lunch I brought on my first day back to school where this afternoon I work with a small group on 12th grade British literature credit recovery. But we aren't getting to 12th grade English any time soon because there's a new guy who doesn't know me, so Hamlet, both the young one and the old one, both living and otherworldly, will have to wait until I pass the pre-test the students give me. *This is the World Peace teacher,* one student says, introducing me to the new guy. And his classmates follow with a string of statements designed to ruffle me. *I've decided I support President Trump,* says another. One adds, *Did you know the Holocaust didn't really happen? The government built fake camps when it was all over.* And finally, another smiles and says, *Your hair is irritating me today. Go fix it. It looks like a witch's hair,* for which I thank him and say, *That's what I was going for.* Because I have taken this test before, I smile, meet his eyes, and say, *Revenge, remember, is it worth it to get revenge? That's what we're talking about. All the ghost wants is revenge, right? Or no?*

Excuses for the Principal

21.

I never told you I hated your surgeon. The one you described as *nice* and *so sharp*. The one who never sat down in the consultation room as he listed the organs he had removed. He stood near the door, arms folded across his clean scrubs.

Your cousin, my cousin, the one who was the principal of my middle school, picks me up from the airport after you're hospitalized again. He takes me to lunch at your favorite restaurant, straight off the red-eye. Another emergency in a string of emergencies. Another phone call. Another flight. *All the principals are dying,* he tells me, rattling names. The names of every assistant principal at every school I ever attended. *Running on two cylinders,* he says. *All of them. Modern medicine is a miracle. A miracle. Thirty years ago, your Great-Auntie fell, and they found cancer throughout her body. She died at 60. A miracle,* he says. *She would have lived longer now. We know so much more.* Miracles or not, the principals crumble.

In fifth grade, I played with Mr. Pull-Apart. A science station in the classroom: a plastic, life-sized torso with a Ken-doll crotch and organs that popped out and back in. I took out his liver, his kidneys, the nubby round of his brain. Putting him back together, if I didn't angle his guts right, his organs would tumble out on the table and I'd have to start over.

I'll have this popped out and be fine, you said before surgery. *Remarkable recovery,* you said months afterward when you could walk on your own again. But you were a principal, pulled apart, like all the others. That surgeon—*so sharp* you couldn't not believe him—never even sat down as my mother wept. All scrubs and scalpel and resected truth.

22.

I tried to tell you about your handwriting, one of the good things you gave me. How so long ago I watched you and practiced, tongue sticking out in concentration at the dining room table. I taught my daughters to make the letter "a" look like typeface and put serifs on the ends like you did when you were writing a card. Crying, unable to speak, you turned away. I stopped trying. I never tried to tell you anything else.

Second Grade Pain

From all of second grade, you remember only the day you had indoor recess. The cute boy picked five girls to do a puzzle at the table. Even in second grade he knew to pick the pretty identical twins. They sang *We Are the Champions* as you hunched under your desk playing with glass animals you had stuffed in your pocket that morning. Even in second grade you knew to act like it didn't matter that you weren't picked. One cold afternoon, so small a thing, but your second grade pain still sings that song.

Idle Hands

Because the principal has established norms for professional behavior, staff meetings feature printed table-tents in school-spirit colors reminding us: no open computers, no side conversations, no grading papers, and no paper-work. My chin slumps into my empty hand as I tap my foot and ape active listening.

I want to declare there will also be no knitting. Despite your smug canvas bag, despite your proclamation there are two parts of the brain and it helps you listen, despite your claims to be a kinesthetic learner, legs crossed, ball of yarn on the floor, you are not listening. Not listening. I know it.

But all I can do is watch your yarn ball twitch as the principal drones on, the projector's glare on the screen the only candle of color under the room's partly dimmed lights.

On Envy

They don't tell you in teacher training that at the end of *The Grapes of Wrath* at least forty minutes of instructional time will be spent on lactation, breastfeeding, and postpartum hormonal changes. The health teacher didn't discuss this during freshman year, and the public health nurse was sick the day she was supposed to come in to demonstrate contraceptives. The future salutatorian, ready to explain what she did learn in health, says, *All I remember is the difference between envy and jealousy.* I used to envy the health teacher with her cartoon bisected penis coloring book pages, her match-and-label vagina parts. Yes, vas deferens, yes urethra, either you know or you don't. Right or wrong. But Rose of Sharon has no label, and the starving man is going to die anyway. Nothing can be corrected at this point. Colostrum, oxytocin, placenta? I wonder about Steinbeck and breastfeeding. He seems to have missed health class as well.

Excuses for the Principal

23.

I told my brother that your hands, near death, looked so much like your mother's if I squinted I could see her gestures. I didn't know I remembered her hands until on the last afternoon you could sit up. You twisted your wrist inward as you emphasized a point. Except for your chemo-blackened fingernails, I could have thought your hands were hers. I looked down at my own hands in wonder. Later, after words had left you, I held your hand and waited.

24.

My mother told me that after your diagnosis, you spent hours in the garage creating photo collages for your funeral. You even counted the photos of the grandkids, so none would be jealous. And you were right, the grandkids counted the photos themselves.

Even the waitress at the post-funeral reception noticed.

She asked, *What did he do?*
I said, *He was a principal.*
She said, *That's why everything's so organized.*
All I could say was, *Yes.*

You told the oncologist at an interview for the clinical trials, *I have so much to live for.* Every bit of it tidy and perfect, arranged behind glass.

The Pile

Once it was a desk. Then accretion, sediment. Layers, a little at a time: quizzes from third period, coffee stain, confiscated kick-me post-it taken from someone's back, and the tardy slips. Hundreds of tardy slips. Answers in handwritten scrawl. An administrator's idea: have the tardy students write explanations for their tardiness.

Why were you tardy? Woke up late.
What can you do differently next time? Wake up earlier.

Why were you tardy? I was fighting evil.
What can you do differently next time? Let evil consume the earth?

Why were you tardy? Waiting for my sister as usual.
What can you do differently next time? Leave my sister behind.

You aren't sure what to do with them, so you stack confession on confession. In pastel triplicate, they are your best excuse for that lost form the administrator's asking after. The one you'll sign just for someone's filing cabinet. The form you have to initial 32 times before you will be allowed to proctor the test. The one that says you'll forfeit your teaching license if you do something wrong on test day.

Where is the proctor agreement? It's in here somewhere. I promise.
What can you do differently next time? I'll clean my desk.

The Proper Use of Frost

Afternoon rolls gray across the stubble of winter corn fields, and your house is the very last stop, so you press the side of your fist to the frosted bus window. Mark toes with your fingertips. Make two right feet and put the big toe on the wrong side. You don't notice you're wrong. You don't consider the bus driver in his nylon jacket navigating the seats at the end of the run, your footprints in negative covering every window. He leans to check behind each seat for stragglers, his boots grinding the floorgrit, leaving nothing behind.

I See His Ghost during the Passing Period

—for J. C.

From the back at first. His blonde hair. His walk. He doesn't wear a vest like the picture on the memorial plaque outside the JROTC room. The boy I see is the boy before he wore the uniform, before the Ranger beret, before three tours in Iraq, before small-arms fire killed him on his second tour in Afghanistan.

I almost say, *Hi, J.,* expecting him to turn and flash the crooked smile of a boy who doesn't have his rough draft done. The one whose hair was too tousled to look military until the day post-graduation, pre-basic training, he dropped in to say goodbye to his teachers. Before I can say anything, he disappears at the corner where the autistic boy with two teacher aides has a room to himself, a room with a rocking chair and a padded mat. The screaming room, my first period class calls it.

On Wednesday, in front of the door to the screaming room, I stand frozen as students flow around me in the five-minute rush, each one unfamiliar, each one already gone.

A Teacher Playing a Movie Star Playing a Teacher

One class, five students, dangerous charm. Each student as beautiful as my too-expensive shoes, which unlike my shitty car, gleam. Look at my car, look at it turn into the empty parking lot in front of a foggy sunrise over a football field. Look at it under the streetlight, the bumper sagging.

Nothing about me sags.

Midnight, juggling keys and folders, a tight shot of my shoes, the click on wet asphalt. When the gang member leaning on the fence straightens himself, think, *Here it comes.* Let his hoodie make you fear for me. Look at the circle of pale light over my car, darkness exiled to the corners of the lot. When he pulls out a notebook, exhale.

Montage: pencils, a tongue poked out in concentration, crossed Chuck Taylor's tapping underneath a desk, reluctant smiles, chipped-nail-polish fingers shuffling cards, dirty-nailed thumbs flipping through a thesaurus. Eyerolls. Balls of paper flung into the industrial can, every wrist a different shade of brown.

My pale hand marking papers in red. Handwritten, blue pen. When I read about the fat girl's rape, zoom in on the heart-dotted "i."

I break up a fight in the hall, hold a boy against the beige cinderblocks using only my voice, the word *fuck* betraying my rage. The principal lurks, arms crossed, belly rising between the flaps of his coat, but he doesn't correct me.

Of course, I cry when the student is shot. Of course, I cry when her father hits her. Of course, I cry when the A+ student is detained. For the obese school board president, I have no tears. I hold my marble-smooth jaw high. On the way out, for once my shoes don't clack, muted by carpet and the applause of the placard-holding crowd in the back of the board room.

Later, alone at the kitchen table, a half-empty bottle of wine. A text from my husband saying he's not coming home. Ever. I'm the only one surprised.

Montage two: backs of my heels, red leather gleam, my bony white ankles, the PTA president smearing her mascara. The preacher, sharp-suited, shaking his head. A framed certificate, a plastic apple, a coffee mug, a brown file box. A hug even from the bitter teacher next door. Empty hallway. A look back at the shadows as the safety-glass door swings shut behind me.

I punch the steering wheel, ugly cry, which for me is still pretty. My car almost doesn't start. Almost. Rattling, I signal and turn left out of the lot.

No One Takes Attendance at Commencement

There's nothing left to do but pay attention to this moment: polyester gown, high heels, the rustle of plastic static. Now is the pinch of bobby pins, the indignity of folding chairs, a breath in, a breath out, a couple of steps, the smooth of palm on palm, the rumpling of paper.

Some call this simulation an end, some a beginning, but it's neither. Neither a door closing nor one opening. It's not the scratch of the pencil's x negating another day.

It's in the steps, in the motion of go, in the bent knees, the swing of an arm. It's in the moment between the bud and the leaf. The moment for which we have no word.

When they ask about the future, don't answer. There is no end and no beginning. If you are present, you are never, ever late.

Excuses for the Principal

25.

You told me that I didn't cry when you held me. I was holding my first daughter, nursing; she'd been crying, so my mother declared, *She has colic just like you did,* and went outside to smoke. I didn't believe you. Every story of my babyhood painted me screaming, so I couldn't imagine my small self as anything but. *No,* you said. *Your mother was so nervous. I think it made you nervous too.* I never told you I was nervous on my own though. You didn't know because I worried I made you nervous. I taught myself not to cry and learned to swallow my nerves instead.

26.

I never asked you if I could read to you in hospice. You couldn't have answered. You lay with your eyes shut, moaning now and again. My mother said, *He always loved your voice,* so I decided to read from a book you loved which I'd never read, *The Count of Monte Cristo.* My brother ran to the bookstore, brought back the book, booklight, and fresh batteries.

Next to your bed, on the side away from the hum of the motor attached to your NG tube, on the side near your Foley bag, where the nurse fussed and measured so often, I pulled up the chair, tucked my feet into the bed rail and used my bent knee to hold the book. Beginning at the beginning, there was time before I had to break the unbroken spine. Sometimes I rested, lay on the couch. Sometimes I paused and watched the lump of you under the blankets.

The last page I read aloud before you died was the moment Edmond Dantès first hears the voice of Abbé Faria after years of isolation.

We were alone in the room. You, your back toward me. Me, toes on the hospital bed, book on my knees. I said, *I'm going to take a break now, Papa. I'll read again in a bit.* I lay on the pull-out cot and watched the splintered afternoon light shift on the wall above your bed.

When my mother returned from smoking outside, I stood to check you, but you were gone. We whispered back and forth above your body before we called the nurse, neither of us able to form more than two syllables: *Is he?*

.

You and I never made it to the part of the story where Faria's death sets Edmond free. Once you left, I set the dog-eared book aside. Left the corner turned down on that page and never picked it up again.

On Tuesday before Third Period They Are All Beautiful

Especially the ones who do not think they are beautiful. The girl hunched in the heavy coat. The boy with acne hidden under bangs which hide his eyes. Even the mean one. Even the one who came to fifth period stoned. Even the one who's too tired to sit up today. Every semester in a writing exercise practicing extended similes, they will write *school is like jail* and believe no one has said it before. At sixteen, they discover sadness, but like seedlings, they can't help but turn toward light. Unlike me, who years ago turned away so hard I turned on myself instead. These days, my sadness, simplified with age, just wants out of these tights and skirt, wants a nap, wants something more than sore feet, tired eyes, ink-stained fingers. Years ago, in 11th grade English, I propped a book on my desk and rage-read while eavesdropping in the background, so when Mrs. Warning called on me to call out my inattention, I could answer defiantly. Years ago, I was the girl hunched in a coat, covering a body I hated more than geometry. This afternoon, that same girl is here, skipping lunch, reading in the corner of my classroom as she peels her chipped nail polish and waits for another bell to ring. I want to give that girl my eyes, let her see herself outside her skin. If only she could borrow them long enough to see the ring of light still clinging to her from the world before.

Notes

The poems in "Four Poems My Incarcerated Students Assigned Me" were inspired by writing assignments I gave my students. Because students are less resistant to writing when a teacher writes along with them, each time I give an assignment, I do it as well. These poems were inspired by writing exercises students chose after reading the work of Natalie Diaz, Sandra Beasley, Brenda Miller, Patrick Madden, Lee Martin, and Peggy Shumaker. Special thanks to Dinty Moore, the editor of the *Rose Metal Field Guide to Flash Nonfiction,* for providing access to a group of excellent prompts that work well for teens. Thank you to the students who allowed me to write with them.

Thank you to my daughter for allowing her notes from the lockdown to be reprinted here.

Thank you to Sarah Doetschman for her sharp eye, intellect, and wit. May every writer have a you in their life.

Thank you to David Crouse, Reneé Singh, Laura Volmert, Aeriale Johnson, Naomi Shihab Nye, Robin Feinman, Janis Lull, Katherine Bouta, and Sandra Beasley for reading drafts of these pieces. Thank you to Robert Alexander and Nickole Brown of the Marie Alexander Poetry Series and Dennis Maloney of White Pine Press for helping to bring this book into the world.

Thanks to the teachers who have offered me guidance and support throughout my career, especially my mentor teacher, Deb Vanasse; my classroom neighbor of many years, Katherine Bouta; my first-year teaching sister, Margaret McDonaugh; and to Peggy Shumaker for modeling compassionate teaching to me long before I ever thought to become a teacher myself.

Gratitude always to T. J. O'Donnell, without whom there would be none of this. Gratitude to C & C both. Their wit keeps me ever on my toes.

Nicole Stellon O'Donnell's first book, *Steam Laundry* (Boreal Books, 2012), won a Willa Literary Award for poetry and was the 2018 Alaska Reads selection. She has received both an Individual Artist Award and an Artist Fellowship from the Rasmuson Foundation, as well as a Boochever Fellowship and an Alaska Literary Award from the Alaska Arts and Culture Foundation. In 2014, she served the winter writer-in-residence at Denali National Park. She spent the spring of 2016 in South India as a recipient of a Fulbright Distinguished Award in Teaching. She is presently serving as a Heinemann Fellow. Her poems have appeared in *Prairie Schooner, Passages North, Beloit Poetry Journal, Alaska Quarterly Review, Redivider, Zyzzyva,* and other literary journals. Her essays and commentaries have appeared in the *Anchorage Daily News* and on the Alaska Public Radio Network. She lives in Fairbanks, Alaska, where she teaches language arts to high school students.

THE MARIE ALEXANDER POETRY SERIES

Founded in 1996 by Robert Alexander, the Marie Alexander Poetry Series is dedicated to promoting the appreciation, enjoyment, and understanding of American prose poetry. Currently an imprint of White Pine Press, the series publishes one to two books annually. These are typically single-author collections of short prose pieces, sometimes interwoven with lineated sections, and an occasional anthology demonstrating the historical or international context within which American poetry exists. It is our mission to publish the very best contemporary prose poetry and to carry the rich tradition of this hybrid form on into the 21st century.

Series Editor: Robert Alexander
Editor: Nickole Brown

Volume 23
You Are No Longer in Trouble
Nicole Stellon O'Donnell

Volume 22
Spring Phantoms
Edited by Robert Alexander

Volume 21
Bright Advent
Robert Strong

Volume 20
Nothing to Declare: A Guide to the Flash Sequence
Edited by Robert Alexander, Eric Braun & Debra Marquart

Volume 19
To Some Women I Have Known
Re'Lynn Hansen

Volume 1
Traffic
Jack Anderson